A TREE
STILL
STANDS

A TREE STILL STANDS

JEWISH YOUTH IN EASTERN EUROPE TODAY

Interviews and photographs by YALE STROM

With an introduction by Sonia Levitin

Philomel Books / New York

Acknowledgments

I would like to thank the following people, who helped to make this book possible. First, I thank my in-laws of Krakow, Basia Skapska and Przemek Swiecicki; Eva Klinger of Warsaw; Jerry Kichler of Wrocław; Daniel and Jarmila Kumermann, and Rabbi and Mrs. Chana Mayer of Prague; Emerich Gerö of Brno; Abraham Meyer Braun of Kosice; Peter and Eva Fischer and Irene Runge of East Berlin; Julian and Corina Şerer of Iasi; Josip Levi of Sofia; Davor Salom of Belgrade; David Kamhi of Sarajevo; Vivian Spacapan-Brumini of Rijeka; Endre Rozsa, Andraś Racz, Rabbi Raj, Rabbi Landesman, and Rabbi Schweitzer of Budapest; Robart Lang of Miskolc; and the Waldner family of Gyöngyös. And special thanks to Precision Lab in San Diego, California, for its careful work in printing the photographs. All of these people provided me with invaluable help and hospitality. Second, I thank the following for their assistance in translating the interviews: Vera Eisenberger, Julia Indichova, Mr. and Mrs. Martin Rosenthal, Phillip Philipovic, Suzie Calev, Terri Rabinowitz, Paula Plafker, and Marcia Radu. Last, I express extreme gratitude to all of those in the United States who helped make this book: my agent, Mary Jack Wald; my editor and friend, Paula Wiseman, who helped me steer a steady and focused course; and my family for their love and confidence. Most of all I would like to thank my wife, Joasia. Without her love, insightful translations, and patience, particularly when I was alone in Eastern Europe for many months, this book never would have been possible.

Copyright © 1990 by Yale Strom.
Published by Philomel Books, a division of The Putnam & Grosset Book Group, 200 Madison Avenue, New York, NY 10016. Published simultaneously in Canada.
All rights reserved.
Book design by Christy Hale.
Library of Congress Cataloging-in-Publication Data
Strom, Yale. A tree still stands: The Jewish children of Eastern Europe today/ by Yale Strom. p. cm.
Summary: a collection of interviews in which young people from Eastern Europe describe what life is like as descendants of Holocaust survivors.
ISBN 0-399-22154-9
1. Jewish children – Europe, Eastern – Biography – Juvenile literature. 2. Children of Holocaust survivors – Europe, Eastern – Biography – Juvenile literature. 3. Jews – Europe, Easter – Biography – Juvenile literature. [1. Jews – Europe, Eastern – Biography.] I. Title
DS135.E9A17   1990   947′.0004924022 – dc20   , [B]   , [920]
First impression.

To the memory of the one and a half million Jewish children of the Holocaust

CONTENTS

A Tree Still Stands is a book of many emotions. To read it is to take a journey back in time, to visit lands where once Jewish life not only existed in all its rich traditions, but grew, until its people were a vital part of the whole community. For centuries Jews flourished in the small countries of Eastern Europe. They mingled with the people there, sharing their culture with them and gaining, in turn, new languages, customs and ideas.

But a cloud fell over Europe, and indeed over the world, a cloud so dark that none other can compare. That cloud was the rise of anti-Semitism under Hitler, and with it the murder of over six million Jews. The loss of six million of their number was an irreparable tragedy. Today, less than twenty million Jews populate this entire planet. The death of so many, and in such brutal ways, had many consequences. Most obvious is the result that Jews are now a *tiny* minority. Those who should have lived to bear children and to witness the birth of grandchildren were cut off. Of those who remained, many lost their zeal for a religion that seemed to bring only pain. Others, attracted to the ways of the majority, left their heritage, either out of rage or just because it seemed easier, less stressful and simply more "modern" to leave the old ways.

So it is with many emotions that we see the faces of these diverse and wonderful young people, the Jews of Eastern Europe. There is sorrow in the past that has shaped them. But there is great joy in the fact of their existence, in their beauty and their brightness. Their very lives are a celebration, for without exception, all are descendants of parents and grandparents who somehow managed to survive the Holocaust. They are the seedlings, the strong and beautiful new growth of an ancient and God-loving people.

All children are special. All hold the hope of the future, the dreams of their parents, the beginnings of a new and better time. These children are special in several unique ways. They live as a remnant. They live among people who often think them odd for clinging to traditions like the Hebrew language, Hanukkah celebrations and Sabbath observance. But these children, far from being isolated in their Judaism, are completely in the mainstream. They talk about government and politics as everyday realities, as well as sports, grades in school, and future plans to be dancers, doctors, musicians and technicians. In short, they are like kids everywhere. They want to have fun. They want to succeed in school and in their chosen professions. They want to feel safe. They want to have friends. Like everyone else, they want to excel, but they also want to belong. That is a tough order when one lives in Eastern Europe, and until recently, it has been more than tough — it has been almost impossible. Now, however, the doors of freedom are opening wide. People are able to move about. They can enter professions of their choice. They are allowed to practice religion. And among the Jewish children of Eastern Europe many do claim their Jewish heritage, not only in name, but in action.

Sadly, some of these youngsters never knew their heritage until recently, and they tell of friends who "still don't know they are Jews." Why? Because fear and bitter memories made their parents and grandparents choose silence.

For some, that silence has only recently been broken. Now they are studying, delving — and some are rejoicing — coming to claim a faith that is sweet in its traditions, noble in its aspirations, and steadfast in its devotion to justice and truth.

Sadly, on the horizon, and within their towns, many also see trouble. They fear another rise in anti-Semitism, for as repressive governments withdraw, bullies and hatemongers are also let loose to do their worst. Many of these youngsters vow never to let themselves be intimidated. They are courageous. They will fight for their beliefs. Many other young Jews see Israel as the only land where they can live without feeling threatened. And some have decided that Judaism is simply not worth the price. They will let themselves blend into the larger populations. They will shed their Judaism like an old cloak, no longer useful, no longer wanted.

So we have here a blending of ideas, experiences and opinions. We have in this book a small mirror of the greater community of Jews the world over — those who care, those who dare, those who live their Judaism with all their hearts, and those who will gladly drop the banner and never look back.

In short, they are the true new branches of this great tree of Judaism, and though a branch or two might break and wither, the tree's roots are strong. The tree still stands.

— Sonia Levitin

Introduction   Jewish youth in Eastern Europe today. This topic fills the mind with questions. Yet up until World War II, Jewish life in the eastern part of Europe was as vibrant as anyone had seen. There were schools, clubs, political parties, and Yiddish newspapers, books, and theater. The Jewish population in Eastern Europe on the eve of World War II was about five million. Over fifty years later there are less than two hundred thousand Jews remaining. And today Jewish youth are still struggling with their hopes, aspirations, and confusion concerning their Jewish identity.

My grandparents are from Eastern Europe and if they had not come to the United States in the early part of this century, I realize that I might never have been born and my family might not exist. Having lived here all my life, I have wondered how alike or different I am from the youth in Eastern Europe. I have visited Eastern Europe many times, but never to answer this specific question. So I decided to take a trip and talk to the young people who live in Eastern Europe today.

In twelve weeks, with at least one interview each day, I spoke to several hundred young people, ranging from age seven to twenty; and by the end of my trip I had taken forty-five hundred photographs. I met with these children in their homes, with their friends, in their schools, and at their community centers. I was amazed at their intelligence, patience, honesty, and maturity.

My sense was that many of the children would be reticent about discussing their government, religion, family, and ideals. But in almost every instance, the people I talked to spoke with great candor about their personal lives and spoke out vehemently against their former and current governments. This may have been partly because most of the interviews were conducted in the native tongue of the speaker. Nonetheless, even when a parent was present at an interview and was obviously displeased at what their child was saying, the child did not hold back. And in some instances the parents were so fearful of the border authorities hearing the tapes that they insisted I erase parts of the interviews while they watched. I did erase when asked to do so because I knew their fears were realistic.

But the real challenge of this book was selecting the photographs and interviews that would make it to the book's pages. I consider all the youth I met my friends, each with his or her unique ideas, personality, language, and voice, and my intent in translating and editing was to allow these qualities to come through. Yet I regret that this book could not reflect every interview of my trip, for each was filled with its own pathos and amazement.

Before leaving on my journey from Warsaw to Sofia, I asked myself some questions. Where and how would I meet these kids? Which cities would have greater numbers of Jewish youth? What sort of Jewish identity would these kids have? How would they and their parents accept my work? For those survivors what possible Jewish culture could or even would they want to pass down to their children and grandchildren? What did these youth know about the Holocaust, and would they speak about it? Did they feel there was a future for Jewish life in their communities? Did it seem senseless to maintain and cultivate a Jewish identity in lands that had so few Jews? Were their joys and concerns of everyday life any different from great politicial upheavals of Eastern Europe? Though separated by thousands of miles, foreign languages, and cultures what were the similarities between these kids and their counterparts in the United States? And finally, did American culture have a greater influence on these Jewish youth than their own historical past?

My three-month trek, traveling mostly by train and carrying a backpack, cameras and a violin, was an inspiring trip. I was able to witness the beautiful innocence of youth, hear voices that spoke with sincerity about their hopes and fears in daily life, and understand what it meant to them to be part of the changing tide of history in Eastern Europe. These are young people you will not forget, each a promise of tomorrow.

— *Yale Strom*

EAST GERMANY

When you walk down the oak-lined street that leads to the gates of the Weissensee cemetery, the largest Jewish cemetery in Europe, the calm that surrounds the thousands of gravestones in row after row hints at little of the grandeur of Jewish life that existed in East Berlin before the war. Germany was once home to one-million Jews, but in the aftermath of World War II, only twenty-eight thousand remained. Today 250 Jews live in East Berlin, the smallest Jewish community of any major city in Europe. But still this community is strong and vital, and there is excitement in the air as the possibility of reunification becomes more and more of a reality.

Daniel Reiter, seven years old, lives with his parents and infant sister in the center of East Berlin, close to the only two synagogues in the city. Mr. Reiter has his own business as an importer and distributor of kosher wines and liquors.

My school goes from the first to the tenth grades. I'm in the first grade now. My subjects are math, German, penmanship and drawing, which is my favorite. I'd like to be either a fireman or an officer in the army when I grow up. After school I play sports like soccer and handball. Mostly I like collecting the chestnuts that are on the ground in the courtyard of the youth center. There are so many. I have a chestnut bag in my bedroom closet.

Yesterday we celebrated Chanukah. We made a small oil urn out of clay for Chanukah. We sang, we danced, and we played a game with a small top that we call a dreidle. Then my father gave everyone some chocolates from his store.

Now that the borders are open, in school everyone is bringing in things they bought in West Germany. We have no more problems with traveling; people are living in much more freedom. Many people do want to go to West Germany, but no one knows if they will really have a better life there. But I think it will be better for us all.

I know a little about what the Nazis did. I was with my parents at the Weissensee Jewish cemetery when the president was there speaking about those who died in the war. Afterwards we went to the big synagogue that was destroyed by the Nazis. They destroyed the big cupola that was on top of the roof. Only half of it was left. The Nazis did many terrible things to the Jewish people. They ruined grandfather's leg. Now he can't walk on that one leg.

Daniel relaxing during the Chanukah party being held at the Oranienburger synagogue (left) and Daniel and his father (right).

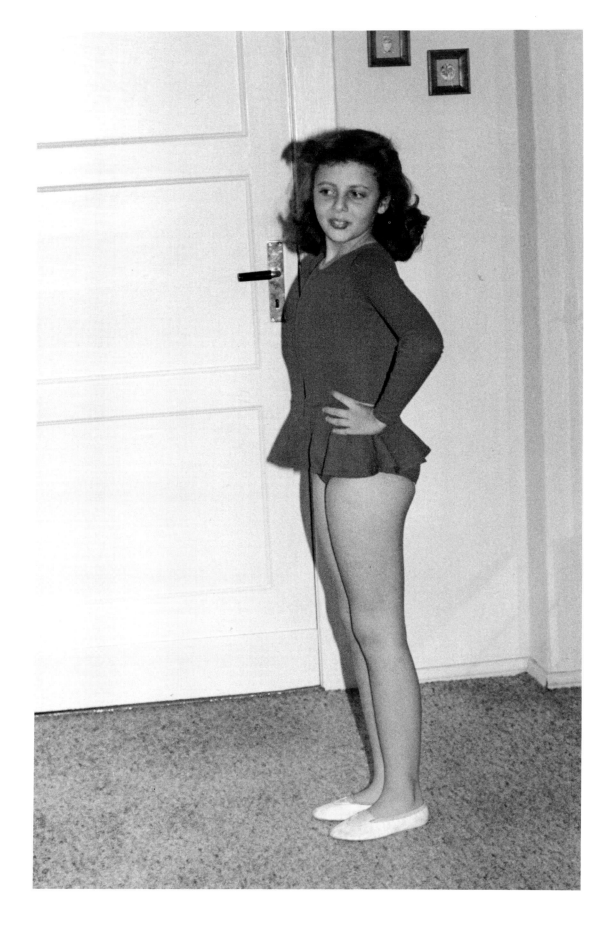

Claudia Lindenberg, ten years old, lives with her parents and younger brother in an apartment in East Berlin. Claudia spends much of her free time studying ballet.

When I will have children I think they should learn about their history. I will teach them about the Jews and how the Jews tried to improve their lives. With my family I would like to visit the Weissensee Jewish cemetery and show them the symbolic grave of my great-grandparents. They were killed in the concentration camp and were not buried. There are many names there, and this is sad.

I really don't understand why the Nazis caused such pain for the Jews. Sometimes I think because the Jews had religious beliefs and thoughts different from Hitler, [the Nazis] couldn't accept them. The Jews wanted a different world, and Hitler didn't like this so he plundered their businesses and deported them to concentration camps. Their children were killed too. I don't think these terrible times will happen again because I read in the newspapers that Gorbachev and Bush work well together. And the capitalistic countries will become socialistic someday.

I went to the wall the night everyone was dancing, drinking, and chipping the stone away with hammers. But my family and I are going to stay in East Germany because it is exciting and maybe soon we will be all one country. I have a friend in my class who walked across the border from Hungary to Austria in September. I will miss her, but now I can travel to West Germany and visit her.

Claudia practicing her ballet at home.

Dörte Luder and Delia Rosenthal are both thirteen. They are best friends and neighbors, and after school they spend a lot of time at the youth center in East Berlin.

Only in the last few years has my father started to talk to me about Judaism. I'm not a believer, but I want to continue the old Jewish traditions in the family, even though I don't understand many of the concepts.

I often go to the Jewish Community Center, especially for the children's afternoon on Saturdays when I can listen to the storytelling. After school I usually have at least one homework assignment, but after finishing it I go over to my friend Delia's and we watch television or go to the youth center. We have lots of friends there.

These days I believe anything is possible. If the Berlin Wall can be destroyed, the biggest change for me will be shopping. I'm looking forward to shopping in West Berlin, even though I'll be doing more window shopping since everything is so expensive there.

— Dörte

Last year I couldn't go to the Michael Jackson or Whitney Houston concerts because we could not travel freely. The changes here have happened very fast and maybe soon we will be one Germany again. But even if the Germanys are incorporated I hope that we don't inherit the same problems they have in the rest of the country, like drugs and unemployment. Why can't we be free and enjoy a good life but not become capitalistic?

I believe Jewish life will exist here in East Berlin when I'm older. There are a lot of Jewish youth who are now going to the Jewish Community Center and that keeps the religion alive. With our new freedom we now have the opportunity to worship and go to religious school in West Berlin. This will help make our culture stronger. But I think that if we swallow too much we can become sick to our stomachs. We must move slowly. We have much to learn.

Today there are still some Nazis living in West Germany, and there is a neo-fascist party in France, but I believe the Jews have learned a lot from the time of their emancipation in 1871 in Germany. Until the Warsaw ghetto uprising, the Jews did not resist. There was a kind of mentality, I believe, not to fight back. That is why it was so simple for the Nazis.

In conjunction with the commemoration of the pogrom night [*Kristallnacht* — the night in 1938 when Jewish stores and synagogues were destroyed by the Nazis], I along with my youth league visited the former concentration camp Sachsenhausen. Some of the former prisoners gave us a guided tour and explained everything. In Sachsenhausen there are two barracks still standing. They were the barracks for Jewish prisoners. I cannot forget them. They were terrible.

— Delia

Dörte (left) and Delia visiting the youth center.

CZECHOSLAVAKIA

As you walk down the narrow cobblestone streets, winding your way past the medieval architecture through the old Jewish quarter of Prague, you suddenly come to the banks of the Vltava River. It was here in the eleventh century that the Jewish merchants traveling the trade routes from the Rhineland to the Near East established a Jewish community, the oldest in continuous existence in Europe. Czechoslovakia as we know it today is made up of the regions of Bohemia, Moravia, Slovakia, Silesia, and Subcarpathian Rus and became a country in 1918. Before World War II some 360,000 Jews made their homes here, but today the Jewish population is about 15,000 (about one-third children) out of a total country population of 15 million. For these people, Prague with its university, synagogues, cafes, and art galleries is a vibrant city, and fervent political action there is slowly transforming the country.

Alzbeta and Klara Mayerova, eleven and ten years old, live in a large, old apartment in the center of the former Jewish quarter of Prague. Alzbeta and Klara are the daughters of Rabbi Daniel Mayer, one of two rabbis in all of Czechoslovakia.

In school I have learned a little about the Second World War and what happened to the people who were sent to the concentration camps. Now we mostly are learning about the Middle Ages.

All my friends at school know I'm Jewish. Being a Jew doesn't make me feel different from other kids. I eat kosher food, sing Hebrew songs and enjoy reading about Jewish history. In my spare time I also like to listen to music. Dvořák and Beethoven are my favorite composers. I don't see Jews as different from anyone else.

— *Alzbeta*

Every second Wednesday we go to Hebrew school, but I wish I could go every Wednesday. There my father teaches us to read and speak Hebrew and about the Jewish holidays. I enjoy drawing pictures most of all at Hebrew school. One of my hobbies is drawing along with reading and running around.

I don't see anything so different about being a Jew, either. I am the same as all the other kids, I'm only a different religion, and I enjoy most of all the Jewish customs.

When I'm older I'm not sure what I want to be — maybe I will work in the zoo. But right now I'm happy just being young, because if I were an adult and went running around in the Old Town square, people would stare at me. Now no one pays any attention when I run around. When I grow up I will have to have better manners.

— *Klara*

Klara and Alzbeta on a downtown street in Prague walking home from school (left) and in the old Jewish quarters (right).

Andulka playing in her backyard after school (left), and Andulka and her mother, Chana, in the family's kitchen after lighting the Chanukah candles (right).

Andulka Pavlatova is an outgoing seven-year-old growing up in a home steeped in Jewish tradition. Her parents have discovered their strong Jewish heritage in only the last ten years.

Now I have no brothers or sisters. I hope to have either one, then I will not be so bored. There are very few Jewish children here in Prague. My friend Helenka is the only other Jewish friend I have.

One of my favorite things to do is read. I enjoy reading the Bible and fairy tales. When I want to be alone and read in a quiet place I go either to a corner in the garden, underneath my bed, or in the clothes trunk.

I like it when we celebrate Chanukah and light the candles or prepare for the Sabbath. Tonight we are celebrating the Sabbath because God created the world in six days and rested on the Sabbath. I learned this from my father who is also teaching me how to read, write and say some Hebrew words. When I will be my mother's age I will celebrate the Sabbath because I like the light that shines from the candles and the feeling of the family being all home together.

My grandmother never speaks to me about her experiences in the war. I learned what happened when we visited the Alte Neue synagogue with my youth club. The Jews had a bad time and had to take many risks. I think the Jews were suppressed because the other people saw them as a different nation and as a bad group of people.

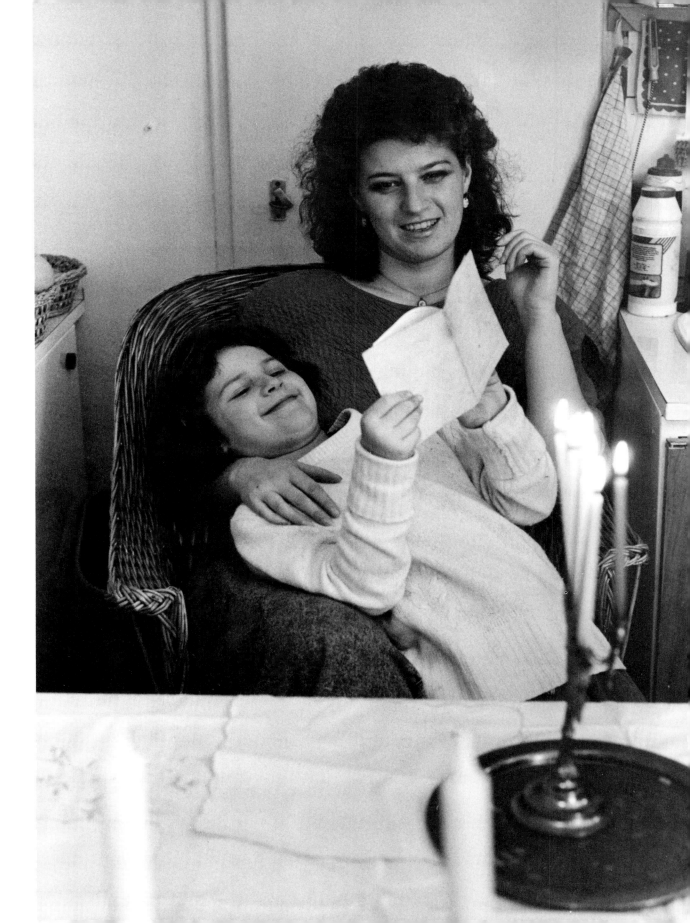

Andrea and Petra Ernyeiova, fifteen and thirteen years old, live in Prague. Their mother is a nurse and their father is a piano tuner who also plays in a Dixieland Jazz band that travels through Czechoslovakia.

I feel Jewish depending upon who asks me, but I am not completely sure if I am Jewish because I come from a family where my father is Jewish and my mother is not. And according to Jewish law that would mean I am not Jewish. I am gradually feeling more Jewish because I have started to understand what it means to be a Jew. A year ago if someone would have said to me, "You're Jewish?" I would have answered, "So what. It makes no difference to me." Then, I didn't understand the meaning of what it meant to be a Jew. But last year our family was invited by the Jewish community in Yugoslavia for a vacation. When I returned I became more interested in my own Jewish identity. Now I am much more aware of my religion.

The Ernyei family, Marta, Ondre, Andrea and Petra at home (left), and Petra and her dog, Ciapek (right).

Sometimes when I wake up in the morning it is hard to believe that what is happening is actually happening. I think the political changes were bound to happen because in the order of the universe something so illogical as our previous government just had to come to an end. Czechoslovakia used to be part of all Europe. There was no need to have such a geographical term as the East Bloc. Such terms were made by a few men to control many. They had everything to gain politically at the expense of the masses.

I think Judaism will have a better chance of survival here in Prague. People before who were afraid to let others know they were Jewish because of a fear of losing or having troubles at their job will not need to fear anymore — at least from the Communists. The Jewish community, especially the youth, will have no excuses now for not choosing to learn more about their Jewish culture.

— Andrea

I don't go to Hebrew school because I don't know much about it. I am more interested in sports. At my school I'm not aware of any other Jewish students. When I am older, I don't think I'll raise my children as Jewish. I would like to live a normal life.

— Petra

David Wichs, eleven years old, is in the fifth grade. He lives with his parents and younger brother in an apartment in Prague.

In Czechoslovakia I don't really feel Jewish. That is mostly because if I tell others that I am a Jew I can make big problems for myself. If I choose to go to a certain high school and if they look at some of my school records and see my absences for the Jewish holidays, I might not be admitted to that high school. There are no Jews in my class at public school and only one other besides myself in the entire school of eight grades. There is one boy in my class whose mother is Jewish, but he does not consider himself a Jew.

Last year in my history class we talked about the Second World War, but my teacher only mentioned the Jews a little. He preferred speaking about the Communists, saying only that Jews died too.

I go to Hebrew school once every two weeks. There are about ten children who attend. We learn to read and write some Hebrew and we talk about our Jewishness. Hebrew school is important to me.

There are not many Jews in Prague because most were killed in the war. Those who survived either married Christians or do not admit they are Jews, because sometimes the word *Jew* is a curse, and there are anti-Semitic jokes. I saw anti-Semitism when I was in East Germany with my scout troop. We were all Czech children. Some of them said "you Jew," and others made jokes against Jews. I didn't like this. These kids probably never met a Jew in their life and thought Jews were some kind of ancient people who lived a thousand years ago. I think these children were probably raised in a bad family. I'll never understand why they said these things.

When I will have children I don't think there will be a Jewish community here in Prague. I hope there will be, but a lot of people want to move out of the country, and we are not so many here.

David getting ready backstage before the Chanukah play (left), and singing Chanukah songs with his Hebrew school classmates in the Alte Neue synagogue (right).

Nicol and Fillip Engelsman, seventeen and thirteen years old, live with their parents and grandfather in a large home in Brno.

It's incredible what has happened here politically. Everyday the newspapers hold something that is exciting to read. We have known for a long time how corrupt our former leaders are, but now we can say it publicly. I am happy to see our new leaders come from outside the party and military. How can a nation respect its government when it governs with force and no compassion? I'm happy for the East Germans but deep down a part of me is worried. A united Germany has only meant trouble for the rest of Europe in this century. And for the Jews how could we want a united Germany?

The Brno Jewish community is a very small one. Most of the people who go to the synagogue are a kind of leftover people. People who survived the war. The majority of them are old. They are slowly dying out, so our numbers are becoming smaller.

I have learned most of what I know about Jewish culture from the almanac, the Jewish newspaper *Vestnik*, from grandfather and father. The borders that define what sort of home we have aren't so distinct. The Jewish part comes particularly from grandfather.

I'm proud of my Jewish heritage and glad I know something about it. I'm not like the rest of the other people who have no idea about their heritage. I belong to the Jews even if it is just a little.

— Nicol

After this year I will go to the Electronics Trade School instead of a regular high school. If I were to go to the high school where one studies everything it would be easier to be accepted into a university. But my father did it this way and became an engineer.

At school or at home I haven't learned anything about what Jewish life was like before the war except that grandfather played leftback on a Jewish soccer team called Maccabi. Though he is short, he was very quick.

— Fillip

*Fillip and Nicol at home with
their sister, Dita (center).*

*Silvia and Karin Krausova, fifteen and twelve years old, live with their
father, a newspaper sports writer, and their mother, a pediatrician, in a
small apartment in Bratislava, the second largest city in Czechoslovakia.*

We have a small Jewish community in Bratislava. But I think there
are many Jews who live among us, who we don't know about. I
have been in the synagogue many times but I don't go regularly.
These days there are only old people that go and pray in the synagogue in Bratislava. It is not an interesting place for young people.
One cannot find anyone young there to get support from. I was in
Vienna this year for a Jewish wedding and there were many people
in the synagogue. I believe Jewish life is better in Vienna than here.

I learned a lot about the tragedy of World War Two from my
mother and grandmother. Grandmother was in a concentration
camp, and I cannot imagine how awful this was. At school we
learned about the Communists who were killed but very little about
the Jews.

The economy isn't very good here, and there are many things one
cannot buy easily. Maybe it will become better here with this perestroika that Gorbachev has made, but I'm not sure. It is easier to
travel now, since Mr. Gorbachev helped to kick out our old regime.
But now we must take control of our own destiny.

If I stay in Czechoslovakia it will only be in Bratislava. It will be
difficult for my children because the Jewish community is so small,
but I feel I must try like my parents have done. I have to believe I
will succeed, too.

— Silvia

I have one Jewish friend. Her parents have not even told her that she is Jewish, but my mother knows her family and has told me. This is very sad to me. One must know who he really is.

There is no Hebrew school in Bratislava. What I know about Judaism I learned from my parents and from the Jewish camp in Pirovac, Yugoslavia, we attended last year. There I learned some Hebrew.

To me to be a Jew means not to feel ashamed of your faith. It is a religion just like any other, and it is very interesting, especially since it is one of the oldest religions of all.

—Karin

Silvia and her mother (left), and Karin at home practicing the piano (right).

Ròbert and Andrea Tesšer, fifteen and thirteen, live with their parents in the center of Košice.

In my school there are one thousand students and only three of them are Jewish—one girl in my grade, myself and my mother who is not exactly a student but teaches German there. I often feel alone.

The future for young people here in Czechoslovakia will not be simple. Sometimes we don't even have some of the basic hygiene needs like toothpaste and toilet paper. So I'm not surprised when there are some things that are not available that we would like to have, like the luxuries. It is difficult here but if you study, your future is much better.

Jewish life isn't strong here. I go to the synagogue once a year with my family on Yom Kippur, because then there are many people there. I didn't have my Bar Mitzvah here in Košice because my mother is a teacher and she could either have some problems or even lose her job if she practices her religion publicly. Teachers are supposed to be atheists. So my Bar Mitzvah was in Budapest.

I would like to be a dancer but my mother wants me to be a doctor, so I have not decided yet. When I'm in the eleventh grade I'll decide.

The changes that are taking place in the Soviet Union now are not changes for one generation but for many generations. You cannot change the Soviet Union in a few months or even years. The Soviet Union can be changed but as they say in Slovak, "You can't tear out the tree with its roots." But their changes are very good. Here in Czechoslovakia for once the changes have happened from the bottom to the top. But I am afraid for us Jews because some people who are quiet about their anti-Semitism because they were afraid of the police, will now be more brazen about their true feelings.

—Ròbert

My grandparents told me about the part of their life they spent in a concentration camp. They almost lost their entire family. It was horrendous there. I can't even look at the photographs from the camp. They are too upsetting.

I would like to have a Bas Mitzvah because I'm Jewish and all the Jewish women, not here but in the United States, have Bas Mitzvahs. They should have them here, but if they can't they can't. Maybe one day we will.

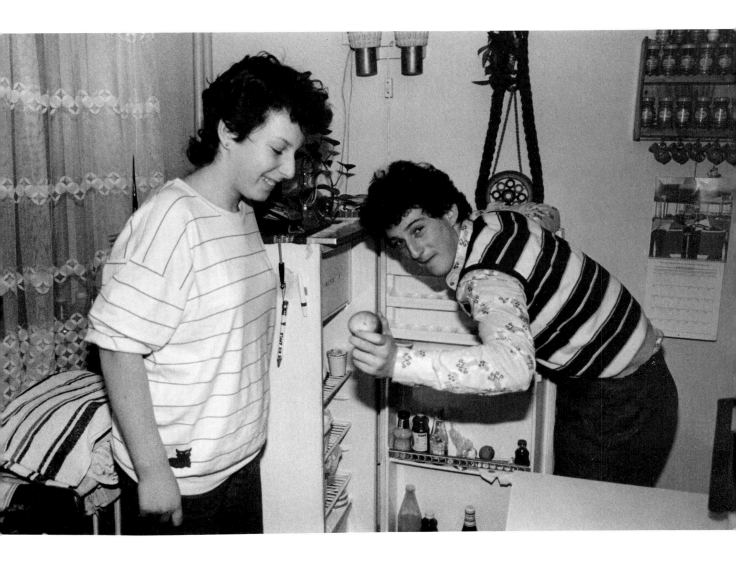

Andrea and Robert helping get dinner ready.

We celebrate many of the Jewish holidays in our home like Chanukah, Passover and Yom Kippur. My father and grandparents have taught me what the holidays and traditions are about. Though we don't celebrate Christmas, I like it because we don't have to go to school and then I get to go skiing.

I would like to be a pharmacist. I know I will have to study in Bratislava and it is far from Košice. But during my studies I think I would rather be on my own because I will have peace and quiet for my studies away from my parents.

— *Andrea*

POLAND

Today when you walk down the lonely streets of Kazimercz, Krakow's former Jewish quarters, and see the busloads of tourists with their cameras, speaking many different languages, you wonder if these visitors understand where they are. Jewish communities have existed in Poland since the tenth century. At the beginning of this century, Poland's Jews were 3.3 million strong and the center of Eastern European Jewish culture. But the Holocaust brought the annihilation of nearly ninety percent of Polish Jews. Today Poland is an anomaly in Eastern Europe. Warsaw is alive with an explosion of Polish-Jewish culture everywhere. Jewish records and books are in every store, posters for Jewish music concerts cover the walls, and lectures and Yiddish theater are common. Poland is an affirmation that some twelve thousand Jews and Catholics are rediscovering an important part of their history — a tattered landscape of their past.

Katarina Katarzyna, seventeen years old, lives with her parents who are both university professors in Wrocław. Katarina is known as Kasia to her friends and family. Dariusz Horszowski, known to his friends as Darek, is nineteen years old. Both Katarina and Dariusz live in Wrocław, the third largest city in Poland.

My home isn't a Jewish one at all. My father is Jewish, but my mother is a Polish-Lithuanian Catholic. My father's parents were Orthodox Jews, but after he left home to study at the university he didn't practice his religion.

I lived with my grandparents until I was six while my parents were studying at the university. It was then that I started thinking about what it meant to be a Jew. How should I act? What should I do? I guess my Jewishness is something inside, an inner space. Something one has to feel regardless of the situation. Whether or not there are Jewish books, Jewish clubs, organizations, these outside things help our individual identity but aren't as important as carrying within yourself proudly your Jewish identity.

Some of my classmates are brave enough to ask me such naive questions as "Do you celebrate Christmas?" It is really incredible how small Polish knowledge of Jews is — and especially since nearly one out of every three Poles before the war was a Jew. My classmates' limited knowledge is unfortunately based strictly upon stereotypes. Recently my friend told me that I destroyed the whole image of what he thought a Jew was. For him a Jew existed as an old man with *payes* [earlocks], a yarmulke on his head and a beard.

I try to understand and appreciate other cultures, so when I am not studying I read a lot about different cultures and listen to reggae music. When I leave the city I like to go rock climbing.

I don't see my future in Poland, but maybe with the new, more positive government a Jewish culture could be sustained. I admire the sense of humor and sense of belonging in the Jewish community. Maybe it is this strong connection with tradition that has held the Jews together and fought assimilation.

— Katarina

I live with my mother who is Catholic, but four years ago I learned that my father was Jewish. After one year of intense soul searching, I decided that I was a Jew, too. I have been called a "dirty old Jew" and a "red-haired Jew," but it is meaningless. Some individuals use the words "dirty Jew" as slander against anyone they disagree with. It offends me and annoys me, too.

I will eventually leave Poland because of the Jewish and economic situation here. The only place I can cultivate my heritage outside the synagogue is at the Jewish club here in Wrocław. It is impossible to really cultivate a Jewish home life here, because at this moment Polish Jewry is dying. It is not dying a natural death because the Jews here are just a remnant of what was once really a culturally diverse Polish-Jewish nation. There are very few Jewish youth my age, and many may leave the country, thus soon there will be nothing.

— *Dariusz*

Dariucz and Katarina relaxing at the Jewish club.

Jakub Lutyk, known as Kuba to his friends, is fifteen and lives with his parents in Warsaw. Though he has been raised his entire life in a Catholic home, Kuba learned last year that his mother's mother was Jewish. His grandmother told this to Kuba's mother just before she passed away.

I wasn't surprised to find out my grandmother was Jewish. My mother has recently begun to search for her Jewish roots, but I feel as a Pole and not as a Jew. I'm a Catholic and I believe in God, but I'm not sure what my attitude toward religion is. Religion for my friends means they feel as Catholics. But in my opinion most of them are atheists.

Depending on where you live in the city, you may or may not encounter anti-Semitism. Once when I was in elementary school, someone called me "you Jew." He used the words in a negative way. It saddened me to hear them. However in my high school people are more intelligent—they would never say such comments out loud.

When I'm not studying, I'm usually playing basketball, going to the movies, taking photographs or listening to music. I listen to punk, alternative rock and heavy metal. I especially like the Polish punk groups like Deserter, Defects of the Brain, Army, and from the West the Dead Kennedys, The Ramones, The Doors and the Rolling Stones.

One of the problems my generation faces is the tremendous amount of schoolwork we receive from our high school. There is a big difference between what we had to learn in elementary and in high school. Everyone I know worries about passing to the next grade, getting accepted to the university and being able to find a job in the profession you choose.

Jakub outside (left) and at home (right).

Justyna Paulak, fifteen years old, lives with her parents in a suburb five miles from the center of Warsaw. Justyna goes to a high school that specializes in English and she, like most of her friends, is fluent in the language.

My father is a Catholic and my mother is a Jew. We don't have an open conflict in the home, but I feel this conflict in myself. I feel I am a Jew. I'm very proud of who I am. But I can't describe myself easily.

I felt lonely in elementary school being the only Jew and hearing other people speak negatively about Jews. But since high school I have made some new friends. In school I only know of three or four other students who recognize themselves as Jews. When I wear my Star of David to school, everyone is interested in it, but that is such a thin way to be a Jew. People don't want to admit being a Jew is a delicate matter. For example, in my elementary school I was afraid to admit who I was because there were so many anti-Semitic incidents taking place. It was nightmarish.

I never spoke to my grandmother about the Holocaust. My mother told me we shouldn't, because it would be too cruel to remind her of it. I remember during the summer camp I went with my cousins to Treblinka. This was a strange experience for me. It was horrible what happened there. I thought a lot about the people that were able to do such things as this. How was one person able to kill thousands? I tried putting myself in the shoes of someone who was able to kill in this way. But I wasn't really able to do so. It seems to me impossible that someone can make such decisions about another people, because we are all humans. We shouldn't have such ideas that leave us to kill other people. It was horrible and unexplainable. So we always have to remember about it and know this kind of ideology should never happen again.

Justyna and her mother in her room (left) and Justyna relaxing (right).

41

Magdalena Klinger, seventeen, known as Piora to her family and friends, is the oldest of three children in a Russian Orthodox home. Her father is a theologian at the state university and her mother is a high school physics teacher; they both were born and raised in Poland. The Klingers live in an apartment in the heart of the former Warsaw ghetto, the place where hundreds of thousands of Polish Jews were confined during World War II before being taken to the death camps. Piora attends a special language school where she studies Russian, English, French and Chinese.

We have many Jewish friends in my home. Even today there is a lot of anti-Semitism among my contemporaries who have never met a Jew or had Jewish friends. In our conversations they can show irrational hatred toward the synagogue. I am interested in what my Jewish friends are doing and I sometimes go to the synagogue with them. Once I was there for a Bar Mitzvah and I enjoyed it very much. I am sorry that there weren't more Jews there, though. Because we were so few, the atmosphere was kind of dead.

I've read many books by I. B. Singer that describe a kind of small-town Jewish atmosphere that is nonexistent today. I wish those times could return. Jews enrich Polish culture. Even though our political situation has changed for the better, I don't believe Jews will return to live here. You can change the government and the economy but this doesn't erase history or the tragic memories. There are only a few Jewish families left, and most of them are not religious. I know only three families who maintain the traditions. Jewish culture is dying here and it's very sad.

Magdalena studying at home.

Justyna Sobolewska, fifteen and a half years old, lives with her father, a film critic, and her mother, a computer programmer, in an apartment in a suburb of Warsaw. Her father is Catholic and her mother is Jewish.

I don't feel especially Jewish because I came to this religion very late, having been raised in a Catholic home. My mother's mother was a Jew by blood but not by religion, and my parents and I are Catholic. Though I have some German in me I don't consider myself German. I still feel Polish. Poland is my home.

In my spare time I like to read, particularly poetry and books by George Orwell. And some of my knowledge of Jewish culture is from the books I read. Recently, as a family we read and discussed a diary written during the Warsaw ghetto. It was sad and intriguing to learn about the Warsaw ghetto uprising. Really, though, most of what I know about Jewish culture is from my grandmother. She often told me stories about her Jewish life before the war. She spoke about the Jews that wore kaftans and had *payes*, or earlocks. I have never seen a Jew like this. My grandmother didn't attend any religion classes when she was young. She was an atheist growing up in a rather well-to-do home that had little contact with Jewish tradition. Her parents were quite assimilated.

When I marry we will discuss about many cultures in my home, one of which will be Jewish. I would like to impart something of a Jewish nature to my children, the next generation.

Justyna and her cousin at home.

The Friedman family, including grandfather and grandmother Friedman sitting next to Marek and Joanna Lea.

Joanna Lea, ten and a half, and Marek Friedman, eleven and a half years old, live in an apartment in Warsaw — with their mother, Catholic, and their father, Jewish, who are both scientists. They lived in the United States for one year and speak fluent English.

I am interested both in Judaism and Catholicism, but I feel Catholic because my mother is Catholic. I go to the synagogue only for special holidays. I go to the church every Sunday.

At home we celebrate Catholic as well as Jewish holidays, like Christmas, Easter, Chanukah, and Sabbath. On Chanukah our parents give us gifts, we eat potato latkes and we light the Chanukah candles. It is a homey holiday but I like Christmas better because it is really a family holiday. On Christmas all our relatives get together.

When we visited America I enjoyed it very much because of the beautiful landscapes and national parks, but I didn't like my school. The school was very easy and boring. I never received any homework and had very few friends. It was good to see America and return to home even though life is harder in Poland. There are long lines and few things to buy in the stores.

My parents work many hours but don't make a lot of money. But of all the professions in Poland, I think teachers receive the lowest salary. I think this is the most important profession in society.

— *Joanna Lea*

I feel rather as a Jew because my grandfather and father are Jews and I think I would like to identify with my father. I'm interested in the languages Hebrew and Yiddish. Grandfather is translating books from Yiddish to Polish and some of them are really fine books.

My favorite holiday is Christmas. On the Jewish holidays we go to see some friends or we stay at home with only the four of us, which is always boring.

I have no Jewish friends so I learn about Jewishness from my grandfather. He taught me about certain things we do on the Jewish holidays. He is teaching me Hebrew for a Bar Mitzvah I might have. With a Bar Mitzvah I will be grown up after the age of thirteen, but here in Poland in the sense of the law one is not considered grown up until he is eighteen. When I'm really grown up I would like to be an astronomer like my mother. It is very challenging to look into the sky and discover new planets.

— *Marek*

ROMANIA

Romanian Jewish life is as diverse as the land itself. Unlike its Eastern European neighbors, where most Jewish communities are found only in big cities, the Jews in Romania live in small towns and villages along the Black Sea coast, on the fertile central plains, and among the forested mountains of the north. When World War II began, Romania's Jewish population of 757,000 was second only to Poland's in Eastern Europe. Until 1972 there were some 100,000 Jews in Romania, but during the twenty-four years under severe rule of former President Ceausescu, thousands emigrated to Israel. Today some 18,000 Jews are feverishly working with their fellow Romanians to rebuild their nation.

Felecia Marcovici, fourteen years old, lives with her parents and older brother in an apartment in Iasi, a university city in the north of Romania. Nearly every day Felecia and her friends go for lunch after school to the kosher restaurant.

At school in our history lessons there were only a few words spoken about what happened during World War Two. Most of what I know is from books, films and what my father has told me. He said that the Jews were considered an inferior race and other people could not stand them. My father with his own eyes saw the pogrom, in June of 1941, that killed thousands of Jews here in the streets of Iasi. This was a very tragic episode in our country's history.

Being around my brother has influenced me a lot. He encouraged me to learn many things about Jewish history and the language. I find Jewish culture interesting and have enjoyed learning more about it. In my spare time I like to go to the movies with my friends. Every Sunday, though, I go to Hebrew school. I have been learning Hebrew since the fall because I need to know it since our family will be moving to Israel at the end of this year. I was in Israel once before, and I loved it. The Jewish community in Iasi is dying. Many Jews are leaving for Israel and other places with better possibilities for an easier life.

*Felecia and her brother at the
kosher restaurant.*

Simona, third from the left in the first row, singing in the choir in the Mare synagogue (left) and the Sere family with Simona's sister-in-law, Corina (right).

Simona Serer, nineteen years old, lives with her parents not far from the center of Iasi. Simona understands Yiddish because her parents speak Yiddish in the home. She just recently graduated from cosmetology school and is currently learning English from her older brother.

Everybody here sees Romanian life in his own way: some with more liberty, others with less. In general Jewish youth my age wish to see themselves in Israel and continue their lives there. Thus I believe in fifteen, twenty, maybe twenty-five years, the Jewish community in Iasi won't exist anymore. It will disappear. Perhaps a sprinkle of old Jews will remain. However I can see why non-Jews stay here. Romanians perceive their lives differently and try to succeed by obtaining an education that will help them seek their own desires here.

When I was in high school, I knew of maybe three other students that were Jewish. Most of my Jewish friends I know from the synagogue, Jewish choir and Hebrew school, all of which I attend quite regularly. I like going to the synagogue listening to the prayers and participating in the happiness of the Jewish holidays and singing in the choir on the holidays. I feel very Jewish, and I'm proud of this.

I'm learning Hebrew because I plan to immigrate to Israel this year. I will miss many things here in Iasi. This is my birthplace where I spent my childhood, the last nineteen years. My family, school, colleagues, friends and way of thinking—I will miss it all very much.

Zenit Marcovic, fourteen years old, lives with her parents and younger sister in an apartment in Iasi.

Zenit and her father in the synagogue during the Purim program (left) and Zenit and her friends eating their lunch in the kosher restaurant after school (right).

Everything in the government here is happening so fast. A generation grew up under the harsh regime of Ceausescu for twenty-four years. He and his followers took only a quarter of a century to take us back one hundred and fifty years. We're so poor that a lemon is worth more than money, because a lemon you can eat and money is only good if you are able to purchase something.

If we truly become a democratic nation then I think some Jews will not immigrate to Israel as fast. I just hope with our new freedom anti-Semitism doesn't come. There are those who are waiting to blame the Jews because Ceausescu treated us relatively well. Some things take more than twenty-four years to change.

If you are Jewish I feel it is your duty to know some Hebrew and maintain the Jewish traditions. And it is especially important for young kids to know what happened to their grandparents and great-grandparents in the Holocaust. To forget the thousands of victims, particularly those killed here in the streets of Iasi, would be shameful and to remember them and continue the culture allows their deaths not to have been without some meaning.

BULGARIA

When you visit the Jewish club or walk by the syna-gogue in downtown Sofia, you can smell the strong aroma of Turkish coffee and hear the chatter of the ladino, or Judeo-Spanish, language. The Jewish community here has a distinct Mediterranean flavor since many of the families can trace their ancestral roots to the Jewish families expelled from Spain and Portugal in the late 1400s. The Jews of Bulgaria were the only Jews in all of occupied Europe to be spared the concentration camps, due to protests by the church, people, and army. Yet by 1950 nearly ninety percent of the population of forty-eight thousand Bulgarian Jews had emigrated to Israel. Today there are four thousand Jews living in Bulgaria.

Myra Arroyo, eleven years old, lives with her parents and younger sister in a large modern apartment her father designed, in the center of Sofia, the capital of Bulgaria. Unlike most Jewish children in Bulgaria, Myra has parents who are both Jewish.

I like the Beatles and Mozart and listen to them all the time. At school I'm in the fifth grade and I prefer math and physics, but I also study history, geography, Bulgarian, German and painting. I would like to learn Hebrew so I can speak with my family in Israel, but I can't now because it would be too many languages for me to learn at once.

It wasn't until I read the story of Adam and Eve from a book of Bible stories that I heard this version of how the world began. It was a very interesting notion to me, but hardly believable. Nobody has ever taken me to synagogue, but I remember Grandmother used to go there. When she is visiting I often hear her speak Espagñol [Ladino–Judeo-Spanish] with Uncle Isaac, but I can't speak it. Grandmother told me some stories about the Jewish holidays and how before the war she would be ridiculed by her friends for going to school on Sunday instead of on Saturday, when everyone else went. In those days they went to school six days a week.

During our history lesson we haven't spoken about the Second World War, but my mother has told me a little about it. I don't want to think about it. It frightens me how they killed the Jews.

Myra, her father, friend Emil, and sister relaxing around the dinner table after supper (top) and Myra daydreaming in the kitchen (right).

Ilia Aroyo, twelve years old, lives with his parents in a new apartment complex on the outskirts of Sofia. Ilia recently returned with his family from West Germany, where his father had a scholarship to study physics for one year.

The changes in my country are not just political but environmental as well. Many people are tired of the dirty water and air. We have to take care of our rivers and mountains since they will be here longer than we will. To me, it is much better not living in the center of Sofia, because here it is quieter and the air is cleaner. But from the other point of view, in the city there are more things to do. When I'm not at school, I like looking at the stars and trying to learn about them and how far they are from Earth.

My mother is not Jewish, but my father is. I have some interest in learning more about Jewish culture. I think it is important to know about different cultures and countries. We rarely talk about Jewish things at home except when my grandmother from Sliven is visiting us. My mother doesn't believe, but my grandmother does. In our home the Jewish atmosphere comes from Grandmother, especially when she cooks certain dishes and tells me about the Jewish history of Bulgaria. She said that during the Second World War there were supposed to have been twenty thousand Jews sent to the concentration camps from Bulgaria to be killed. But the Bulgarian people didn't want it to happen and most of the Jews were saved.

These stories are important to know.

Ilia on his bicycle outside of his apartment.

Simon Felix Koen, six and a half, lives with his parents, who are both Jewish, in the Gypsy quarter of Sofia. Simon speaks Spanish as well as Bulgarian at home. He learned Spanish from his mother, who has lived in Mexico City, Bogotá, and Havana.

I go to the Alliance School where I am studying English. I hope to learn Hebrew, too, so I will be able to speak with people in Israel when I will go someday. I was at a synagogue for my first time yesterday in Samokov. But I don't know what people do in a synagogue. My parents have never taken me.

My grandparents have taught me almost everything I know about Jewish culture. They told me how the Jews were tortured during the Second World War. And we celebrate the Jewish holidays with them. Every year on Rosh Hashanha [the Jewish New Year] my grandmother bakes marzipan cakes for us. They are my favorite.

Simon, his father, Felix, and mother, Aneta, enjoying an early spring day (left), and Simon standing in the only synagogue in Samokov, which is currently under renovation (right).

Evelina and Victorelly hanging out.

Victorelly Francess, known as Victor, is seventeen years old and lives with his parents and fifteen-year-old sister, Evelina, in Sofia.

In general our schools are very bad. We have to learn many things that are not useful to us. The college-entrance exams are difficult, but I hope I will pass. I would like to study electronics or communications and maybe become a computer programmer.

My mother is Christian and my father is Jewish. Since Jewishness is derived through the mother, I'm not Jewish. Most of what I know about Jewish culture I've learned from movies, books, and from my grandparents. My father doesn't get involved in any of this Jewish stuff. He knows about it, but it is my grandmother with her Jewish cooking who has brought Jewish atmosphere to our home. I have passed the synagogue many times, but it never crossed my mind to go in. I've been in churches to see the interior architecture. I'm not religious and generally don't believe in God. I believe there is a force that rules people and there is a certain purpose for everything.

The Bulgarians don't know much and aren't interested in Jewish culture. For them Jewish culture is weak here. But for the Jews, even though they aren't many, the culture is strong because they keep it within themselves. They hold on to their religion because it keeps them together.

— *Victorelly*

I don't feel Jewish. I feel as a Bulgarian. To be Jewish means to be ridiculed and hear such remarks such as other Hitlers are going to emerge and something bad is going to happen to the Jews.

In school I learned about the six million who were killed and the miserable Jewish situation during the Second World War. They were tortured and there was a lot of discrimination against them. Many were sent to the concentration camps, but in Bulgaria, the people succeeded in not allowing the Jews to be deported.

I don't believe in God. I think many more people believed in God before the war, but they became disappointed when he let them down in the moment they needed him most.

— *Evelina*

YUGOSLAVIA

In Yugoslavia, Jews live in all of the six republics that make up the country, and each of these places is unique because of its specific history and culture. The Jews of Skopje, in the rural mountainous republic of Macedonia, trace their ancestry to the Jews of Greece, Turkey, and the surrounding Mediterranean islands. The Jews of urban Zagreb, in Slovenia, trace their closest ancestors to the Jews of Central Europe. But the strongest cultural influences on all of these Jewish communities came from the Sephardic world, via Spain and Portugal. From 1918, when Yugoslavia became a country, until the eve of the Holocaust, the various Jewish communities thrived with a total population of seventy-five thousand. Today, though there are only about seven thousand Jews in the country, Yugoslavia has one of the most active and youth-oriented communities in all of Eastern Europe, second only to Hungary.

*Ranjko gazing at the hills of
Sarajevo (top) and Ranjko and
his friend Rut walking home
from the Jewish Community
Center (bottom).*

Ranko Jajčanin, nineteen years old, lives with his mother in a house in the hills that surround Sarajevo. Three years ago Ranko converted to Judaism from Serbian Orthodox and is now studying to be a cantor.

When people talk about Jewish life in Sarajevo they always talk about "before" the war and in comparison to today. That is because Jewish life here has virtually ceased, given the fact that Sarajevo used to be called "little Jerusalem." That was in the time when one-sixth of the city was Jewish. Jewish life hasn't shrunk but was literally destroyed during the Second World War. Given the size of the community today it is functioning pretty well. In general, religion has always been weak here, but specifically the synagogue after the war has drawn few. Jews who stayed after the war were mostly Communists and partisans, and for the most part weren't religious. Subsequently they haven't brought up their children with any religion.

But I think that slowly more and more people are starting to come to the synagogue. In fact because of the internal ethnic crises more people are going back to religion. I believe that most Jews will come back to their God and religion.

I would neither encourage nor discourage anyone from converting like I did. It is a matter of one's own will and one's own judgment. The differences between religions are becoming more and more negligible and are reduced to different interpretations of the same thing. I think in the overall framework everybody has the right to choose the form of belief they want. With this reawakening of religion, people have started learning not only about the religion they were born into but about other religions as well. People recognize that they belong to the same God and have the same moral values on life. But I believe that until everyone learns what happened in the war the possibility of the Holocaust repeating itself is strong indeed. Another way to prevent this from happening again is insisting that every ethnic group's history, tradition and religion, the whole of life, must be passed on to the next generation.

Aleksandar Cereśnjeś, ten years old, known as Sasha to his friends, lives with his parents and younger brother in Sarajevo.

Math is my best subject at school. I hope to use my skill in math to become an architect when I'm older. I like to play basketball with my friends and on Saturday I go to the Jewish Community Center where I draw, sing, play piano and watch movies. On the different Jewish holidays we participate in various activities at the center. On Purim we make masks, vote for the best mask, then entertain ourselves with games and food. My father is the president of the center, but I don't know what he does there except sign a lot of papers.

Denis Zekić-Ileš, eight years old, lives with his mother and grandmother in an apartment in Sarajevo. Denis often goes to work with his mother, who is the coordinator of all youth activities at the Jewish Community Center.

When I'm at the center playing basketball I like it because I'm the smallest of all the players and I'm very quick.

At home on the Sabbath Mama lights the candles, then she makes a blessing over the wine. I get to finish the wine she doesn't drink, then I make the blessing over the bread. Often for Sabbath dinner Mama makes rice and kale, which I positively dislike. Mama's learning Hebrew now, and I hope to begin soon. Hebrew is a beautiful language and I like it. My mama is my teacher when it comes to Jewish stuff. She told me that in the Second World War the Jews were persecuted by the Germans, the enemy. Many Jews died in the war. We lost some family, too. But Grandma survived. Grandma speaks many languages, German, French and Italian, and they're all beautiful.

I enjoy being Jewish because it means being full of play and good times. It's important to know your religion.

Aleksander (far left) with his younger brother, friend and father enjoying he warmth of the late afternoon sun (left) and Denis and his mother in the backyard of the synagogue (right).

Rut Danon, nineteen years old, lives with her parents and younger brother in an apartment close to the Jewish Community Center in Sarajevo.

I hope to be a piano teacher. I thought about being a concert pianist, but I don't think I have a chance of getting into the school I would need to become a performing artist. I practice six hours a day, mostly classical music and some modern like U2, Pink Floyd and Sting. Sometimes I play and sing Ladino music with a local group.

This Jewish generation of today doesn't have much enthusiasm or many ideas for organizing Jewish activities on its own. It is the middle-aged that have the enthusiasm. Right people, wrong time. The problem is that fewer and fewer Jews know about the Jewish community. Fewer parents bring their children to the Center, and the community is vanishing because we were so few to begin with right after the war. Most were killed. It also has to do with assimilation. My mother could have easily married a non-Jew because that's the way she was brought up after the war. Many Jews did marry outside their faith. And with the advent of the socialist revolution there was no chance for the Jewish traditions to persist. Jewish life before the war was very creative in Sarajevo. There were many associations, music societies, dances, acting companies and even several Jewish newspapers. Unfortunately, I think most of the young people are going to try to leave in the next decade. This community will die out. This is why I definitely feel I need to learn much more now while there are older Jews still living who can teach me. I want to keep the roots of my heritage alive.

Rut and her mother enjoying a quiet moment from the roof of their apartment (left) and Rut and her mother enjoying the view of Sarajevo (right).

Rina, eleven years old, and Elena Brumini, eight years old, live with their mother, a dentist, in an old apartment that overlooks the Italian quarter of Rijeka and the Adriatic Sea.

I go to the Italian school. Learning Italian is very useful here since there are many Italian people who live and work here. We often buy our fruits and vegetables from an Italian woman. In English I can understand maybe every fifteenth or sixteenth word in a book. I'm trying to learn, though it's not going great. My favorite thing to read in English is comic books.

I go every year with my sister to the Jewish camp in Pirovac. There we swim, put on shows, dance, have visual-art groups and journalist groups. It's great fun. But we sing sad Jewish songs that make me feel like crying. Singing these sad songs on the Sabbath leaves me with red eyes. I only like it when we light the Sabbath candles when we have a power shortage. Then it is scary and fun.

We rarely go to the synagogue, and when we go Mom has a meeting and we play hide-and-seek in the large hall with all the seats. Mama is my teacher when it comes to anything Jewish. She reads me stories from I. B. Singer like "The Wise Men of Chelm." My mom also taught me about Jewish history. She told me when the war started, the Jews were taken to the concentration camps and burned. Everyone should know this happened, even the non-Jews, so this tragedy couldn't happen again. Otherwise all humanity suffers and dies. Our Jewish community is getting smaller. Some of the people are giving up, and no new people are coming to take their place.

— Rina

The best thing I like about school is when I'm not there. The teacher I have is crazy. During my free time I love to read comic books, short and long stories, and Jewish stories from the Bible. For a couple of weeks in the summer I go with my mom and sister to Pirovac. I like it there because there are many folklore groups to choose from. One of these folklore groups is dancing. I love dancing and would like to be a ballerina when I'm older.

— *Elena*

Rina on her favorite getaway her rooftop (left) and Elena (right) doing her homework.

Nikola Radič, eighteen years old, and Djordje Kaurin, seventeen years old, live in Belgrade. Nikola spends a lot of his free time working on his painting and photography. Djordje plans to study electrical engineering after high school.

Nikola and Djordje going out one evening.

My grandma and mother were baptized, but in those times it wasn't very significant. I received most of my knowledge about Judaism at home. We're not very religious, and there aren't many opportunities to practice one's faith. I didn't have a Bar Mitzvah, but I would like to have one someday. Most of my insight about Jewish culture comes from the hundreds of books I've read, everything from Moses to Golda Meir.

Jewish life has been dying out here for forty years. This is understandable because of the politics of the country, the war and because a lot of people moved to Israel, especially in 1948 and in the fifties. Another reason for its demise is the politics of this country which are quietly but steadily working against any religious revival. It is much more practical to be a member of the party. You get privileges in getting a job and an apartment. You can't participate in the party if it is known you are practicing religion.

Recently Jewish life has begun to improve, though I'm not sure it will last for another generation. It's up to the next generation to make their own choices.

— Nikola

I'm only one-eighth Jewish, on my mother's side, but that's enough to make me feel Jewish. In my home the Jewish traditions weren't considered very important.

Jewish religion is weak in Yugoslavia because many parents have given up on the religious traditions and have switched to other things, such as being members of the Communist Party. But recently in the past few months many more Jews are beginning to come to the synagogue with other people in this country beginning to search for their heritage. There isn't a Yugoslav nation as such and many people are looking for their ethnic roots, including their Jewish heritage. Many Jews now realize that their parents haven't done much in regard to giving them a strong Jewish identity, so the young have to seek for it themselves. Generally speaking these Jewish youth are active but not so much into religion. They're interested in other things like traveling and politics in the Jewish community. But better some Jewish cultural growth than no growth at all.

— Djordje

Viktoria, eighteen years old, lives with her mother in an apartment near the center of Pest, close to the Anna Frank Jewish High School.

I still cannot fully accept the fact that I'm Jewish. I'm proud of it, but I'm afraid too. Not of the responsibility, but of the lack of trust the Hungarians have for the Jews. I feel some kind of danger. Even if something is not the Jews' fault, they still doubt them. I have yet to accept my Jewishness fully.

I'm not sure yet about going to college, but I plan to keep active in various sports, especially gymnastics, my favorite, after I graduate from high school. I just won a gold medal in the Hungarian Gymnastics Championships in the youth category. My mother is a coach, and I was sort of born in the gym.

In 1956 the Jews didn't belong anywhere, neither to the working class nor to the ruling class. They were the so-called entrepreneurs, they were just "hanging" in the air. Now we belong somewhere. This is very important. Here at my high school we learned about the Second World War. Our history teacher included a special thesis about the fate of the Jews on our finals. It is very important to know what existed before the war and why it is not present today. Of course we have to learn about world history, too, but for me our history is the most significant. The film of Anna Frank's diary was very influential for me. Seeing her life made it that much more real.

Viktoria practicing her gymnastics at the Anna Frank High School.

Jovan, his father, and Andreja (left to right) discussing a point about basketball.

*Jovan and Andreja Verber are eleven-year-old twins who live with their
parents in an apartment underneath the synagogue in Belgrade.*

My grandfather has been my teacher of Jewish culture at home. My
grandfather is a Jew and because he passed this knowledge onto
me, I will pass it on to my son. I don't think Jewish life will be quite
the same when I'm my father's age. I don't think we will meet as
often as we meet now at the community center. Now we meet every
Saturday.

My grandfather told me about the Second World War, and I don't
think something like this could ever happen again. I don't think
man has a desire to conquer the world and persecute according to
their race.

In my school of about three hundred my brother is the only other
Jewish person I know. I'm glad I don't have a sister because my
brother sometimes gets on my nerves.

— Jovan

I like school because I can spend more time there than I can at
home. At school I like all my studies, but I especially like biology
because I like learning about my body and plants. In my free time I
go anywhere where my parents aren't.

My Jewish studies are with my grandfather. He often tells us
stories about the Second World War. He has told me and my brother
how his parents were killed by the Nazis and how a non-Jewish
friend helped him escape and saved him during the war. He has
also told us stories about famous Jewish people. One of these is
Moses, who is my hero because he made the great effort to free the
Jews from slavery. At Grandfather's and Grandmother's we celebrate the Jewish New Year and Grandmother buys us presents.

When I'm my father's age I'm not sure how Jewish life will be. But
I guess that my generation will pass our traditions on to the next.

— Andreja

Dina Djurovic̀, eighteen years old, lives with her parents in the heart of downtown Belgrade. Her mother, born in Madrid, and her father, born in Sarajevo, are Sephardic Jews. Dina goes to a high school that specializes in languages and is learning English and French. Her English is fluent.

I spend most of my free time with the choir performing and rehearsing. I haven't been singing long in the choir, about half a year. My mom has been singing there for over twenty years, and is the head of it, so it's been a part of my life since I've been born. Most of the Serbian-Jewish Choir doesn't know Hebrew. There are only about ten or eleven Jews who are really interested in knowing what we're singing. The rest are totally indifferent and approach each song in the same way.

I have to admit that in our home we really haven't observed the Jewish rituals very strictly. But I knew from early on that I was growing up in a Jewish family, that we are Jewish. My close friends aren't Jewish. But I feel as Jews we have some themes that I can't discuss even with my best friends. We have common interests specific to the Jewish youth only. And we talk about things that for others may seem silly but for us are important.

Among Jews and non-Jews we rarely speak about the Second World War. It's a sensitive subject. You learn about the war and Hitler, but in Yugoslavia one doesn't talk about it. Half the country was on Hitler's side and many people who are in prominent positions today persecuted the Jews. Sixty thousand Jews were killed, shot and burned in concentration camps in Yugoslavia; these facts are simply not mentioned. As a result the Jewish population in Yugoslavia is small today. There are about three hundred young Jews registered with the Jewish Community Center in Belgrade, and about twenty of them regularly come to the center. This means the youth aren't particularly organized. Some even don't know where the center is, but we who are coming are having a great time.

People are completely uninterested in religion, both Jews and non-Jews. Partly it's society's fault, because they haven't been nurturing traditions. The Jewish religion wasn't banned but sorely repressed. I admit I want to know much more about Jewish religion. Today Yugoslavia is a state where the nation is everything. Everybody wants to know their heritage. It is precisely because of this that these cultural ethnic groups are forming. So who knows how Jewish life is going to look like in ten or twenty years?

*Dina and her boyfriend walking
to a movie.*

Jelena silhouetted against a mosque (left) and at Israeli folk dancing practice (right).

Jelena Coloric̆, thirteen years old, lives with her parents in an apartment in a suburb of Belgrade. After high school Jelena wants to go on to the university to study computers.

My mom is Jewish and my dad Serbian. Our home is a combination of Jewish-Serbian traditions. My mother makes special Jewish dishes for some of the holidays and celebrates Passover, Yom Kippur, Purim, Chanukah and Succoth at home and at the synagogue. My dad cooks many traditional Serbian foods at home that use a lot of meat that Jews aren't supposed to eat. I particularly don't like meat of any kind that much, so I don't eat Dad's cooking.

Every year after school is finished I go for summer holidays to the Jewish camp at the seaside of Pirovac. There I meet Jewish kids and adults from all over Yugoslavia. Every year on the first of May we have a Maccabia Games, a kind of Jewish Olympics, where Jewish youth from all over Yugoslavia and from some other countries compete in various sports. This year my mom thought I was too young to go by myself, but next year I plan to attend and participate in the sitting-down sports like card playing and chess.

HUNGARY

The Jews of Hungary constitute the largest and perhaps the most vibrant Jewish community in Eastern Europe. When you walk the streets of the former ghetto you can see people buying and selling at the Jewish gift shops, kosher butchers, and bakeries. You can hear the chatter of people as they walk to the Jewish museum and various synagogues where children practice their Hebrew lessons and sing in the Jewish choir. The Jews originally came to Hungary as slaves of the Roman legion that conquered most of Central and southeastern Europe, and through the centuries the Jewish community grew and prospered. On the eve of the Holocaust, Hungary had a Jewish population of about four hundred thousand. Today about one hundred thousand Jews live in Hungary.

Tibor Waldner, fourteen years old, and his sister, Edina, nine years old, live with their parents and father's mother in a house in Gyöngyös, a small town fifty miles east of Budapest. The Waldner family represents half of the Jewish community of Gyöngyös, which totals ten people.

I really enjoy sports, especially kung fu. Kung fu is good for both my physical and spiritual self. I also play the guitar and sing with my friends. Our specialty is Heavy Metal, with such groups as Killer, Metallica, Andromeda and Motor Head being some of my favorites.

I'm the only Jew at my school, but I don't feel it as a disadvantage. I fit into the group and have friends at school. Once or twice some guys teased me about my religion, but I took good care of them. I beat them up. And now there is no racism.

From books I've read on my own, I've learned a lot about Jewish history. In 1944, they deported the Jews from here. I think there were about six thousand. Few returned. The Jews from the small towns were taken first to the ghettos in Budapest, then they were sealed in trains, beaten and taken to the death camps. This history is extremely upsetting and shocking to me.

— Tibor

Grandma and Grandpa talked about the Second World War, and I learned a little from the TV. What happened to the Jews was very shocking for me. If this were to happen again, this time we would have to get together and prevent it, and not wait for outside help.

From my parents I've learned a little Hebrew. We have a small book at home and Mom and Dad teach me. Learning Hebrew helps me when I go to the big temple in Budapest, the Dohany. I like it very much that there are still people who go to the synagogue and dare to believe in God and pray. When I'm there I pray that there will be a good harvest and that the bookstore Mom is a manager of will prosper.

— Edina

Edina (left) and Tibor and his mother in the Jewish cemetery after visiting the grave of Tibor's grandfather (right).

Zoltan Elek, fifteen years old, Tamàs Freund, fourteen years old, and Robert Láng, fifteen years old, live in Miskolc, an industrial city east of Budapest with a community of three hundred Jews in a population of 200,000.

I am happy here, even though this is a pretty filthy city from all the air pollution. There are a lot of factories here. Someday I'd like to move to Budapest, and if I like it, I'll probably stay. In Budapest I think that Judaism is more serious stuff. They have more Jews, rabbis, synagogues, kosher butcher shops, even a Jewish high school. Here in Miskolc, we have nothing like that.

It was my grandmother who first taught me some Hebrew and Yiddish. She used to live in our home and she was very religious. I'm glad she spoke Yiddish because it has helped me with my German lessons in school. I miss her.

— Zoltan

My grandfather was quite a religious and knowledgeable man. Sadly my father wasn't able to learn from him, because Grandfather died when Father was young. There are so few religious people here, but we are trying to keep up the tradition. I think there will be Jews here if we raise our kids here the same way our parents have raised us. As the rabbi told me yesterday, we are heading down the slope of Jewish culture and we are the ones who are capable of stopping this slide.

When I graduate high school, I thought about being a cab driver like my father. But nowadays it is hard to make a living as a cab driver. People don't have the money to take a cab and don't have the money to buy a car. So I'll stick to my skill and try to make a living as an auto mechanic.

— Tamàs

I don't have any desire to move from Hungary. I believe once you are born here you should die here, too. We do have many problems here. I live in Miskolc, which is to say, my life is pretty boring.

At school I learned about the Second World War, about the tortures and millions of people having been murdered. I feel, however, that because the teacher was not Jewish he cannot feel what a Jew feels. How can they really understand these pictures of Auschwitz, its tortures and murders? The teacher just stated the numbers of those murdered and other facts coldly.

My parents told me that before the Second World War there were about thirty thousand Jews in Miskolc. Now we barely have three hundred, and not even all of them come to the synagogue on the High Holidays. And there are even fewer young Jews. After us comes the flood, as in Noah's ark. I think there is not going to be anything here in twenty years. The old people will die, and they are actually the only ones who keep the spirit here.

My grandfather talks about the war all the time. He was not killed. I think it must have been a terrible, terrible thing, first to survive and then to live with all those memories. That is another thing entirely, isn't it?

— *Robert*

Tamas, Robert, and Zoltan (left to right) sitting on the entrance steps of the synagogue on warm spring day.

Andrea relaxing at home.

Andrea Legradi, sixteen years old, lives with her parents and older brother in an apartment in the Buda hills overlooking the Danube.

I think Jews must learn about their history. Learning and knowing about what happened to the Jews in the Second World War is very important for the future of Judaism. It must not be forgotten, so something like it will never happen again. I think that every young Jew in the world — from America to Brazil and from Poland to Israel — must go and see the concentration camps, understand what happened and live their lives accordingly.

I participated in the March of the Living last summer in Poland. For me it was the first time I felt connected with Jews from all over the world. We have never seen such a gathering in Budapest ever. It was fantastic. We went through several concentration camps. Everyone had an incredibly horrible feeling inside themselves. I can't really talk about it, it was too horrible.

I believe when someone is born a Jew, he should stay a Jew and not assimilate. If our ancestors who survived the Second World War, despite all the suffering, have the strength to live a Jewish life and raise a new generation, then we cannot break off our heritage. Some years ago many Jews were ashamed of their religion and they didn't want to publicly admit that they were Jews. Today there is more freedom in practicing religion. With the recent political changes more and more people are sending their children to Jewish activities. And it is not only the Jewish people but Christians who are becoming more visibly involved in their church as well. I think Jewishness isn't only the Jewish religion, it is a sense of community. There are many examples in Jewish history when the sense of community could have been destroyed, but the Jewish people cannot be torn apart. I'm a Jew in the first place, then a Hungarian Jew. In other words I'm not a Hungarian who is a Jew but a Jew who is a Hungarian.

Szilvia Dötsch, eighteen years old, lives with her mother in Budapest.

We just moved here last year from Szolnok, which is a small town south of Budapest. I wanted to be with Jews my age and live as a Jew, and it was difficult in Szolnok. There are only about seventy Jews there, and some of them do not even know they are Jews. I was the only Jew in my high school. When I was in primary school, some kids began bothering me just because I was Jewish. My mother said be proud of your Judaism. And from then on I have had a strong Jewish identity. My grandfather is a Jew, and so is my mother, but I don't have any other living relatives because of the Second World War. Many Jews today didn't know they were Jewish until they were young adults. It is hard for them now, and being Jewish I understand them a bit better.

Now many parents don't have any idea about religion, and it is their children who teach them. It wasn't like this for me. After my grandmother died, I went to live with my grandfather for ten years. He was Orthodox and he was my teacher. We need more knowledgeable Jews who can teach us in high school, especially about the Holocaust. It's not the same when a non-Jew teaches us. You must feel it to be able to teach it. My grandparents met in the concentration camp in Tukheim, Germany. After the war they married. I'm lucky just to have them. Through their horrifying stories I felt the Holocaust.

I personally don't believe in God, but I believe in my Judaism. I'm a Jew and I'm proud of this. I don't say there is no God, but after the Holocaust one can understand my doubts. I just don't know.

Szilvia and a classmate taking time off during a literature lesson (left) and Szilvia at a children's park near the Anna Frank High School (right).

Agnes Kardos, eighteen years old, lives with her parents and younger brother in Budapest. Recently Agnes returned from having lived in Göteborg, Sweden, where her father, a Reformed Rabbi, lead the Jewish community.

I go to the Anna Frank High School, which is a Jewish high school, because I was worried I might encounter discrimination at a regular high school. After all, we are all Jewish at the school. After school when I'm not helping my mother or father, I like to jog.

Jewish life is growing here because now it is less dangerous to be religious. Lately it has become even a bit exotic to be outwardly Jewish. These are important times. The government is looking more towards Israel, and Jewish cultural life is becoming stronger and stronger. There are Jewish dance groups and sport groups. Today to be Jewish doesn't necessarily mean only going to the synagogue. Unfortunately with Jewish culture growing, anti-Semitism is growing too. Before the war there was a soccer team that had a few Jewish players. Today it is almost impossible to see this team play because all the terrible exclamations you have to listen to during their matches. And it is kids who are saying these slogans. I can't believe these comments are brought from their homes.

It is important that everybody knows about the Holocaust, so it is known around the entire world. And with this knowledge the Jews will have learned that whenever they get into trouble they can only rely on each other. During the war there were too few who came to the Jews' rescue. They had to survive it alone. Despite the Holocaust my feelings on life are like those of Anna Frank and how she liked to see people. She wrote in her diary that whatever was done to her, she still was capable of loving people. I think this is a very nice thought.

Agnes and her brother Peter waiting for the tram (left) and Agnes and friends enjoying a Sunday afternoon of Israeli folk dancing.

Judit, Katalin, and Agnes (left to right, center row) with friends outside after their choir practice.

Agnes Sommer, sixteen years old, Katalin Ebner, known as Kitty to her friends, fifteen years old, and Judit Klein, fourteen years old, live in Budapest and are all good friends. Every Sunday they sing together in the choir at their synagogue.

When I'm not in school or coming here to the synagogue or singing or any other activities, I'm busy with basketball practice and matches.

Hungary is becoming a more open country and is cultivating stronger connections with Israel. I think the youth, both Jewish and non-Jewish, don't know everything about the Holocaust and these terrible things. They want to learn, but I don't think they can fathom the historical reality of such an event. Though my mother isn't Jewish, we have a Jewish home. And I think when I marry I will have a Jewish home because it is important to have harmony in the family.

— Agnes

I have been in this choir for four years. It is good fun, and I enjoy the company. It is familylike. We also go to many places abroad and give concerts. This summer we will travel to Israel for a concert.

I rarely go to the synagogue, but I would like to get to know my religion better — so perhaps I will begin going on a more regular basis. When I am married, I will have a Jewish home for my children. There is no question about it. They must know where they belong as a people and not just "hang in the air."

— Kitty

Next year I will attend the Anna Frank High School, which is a Jewish high school. The school is smaller, feels more like a community, and your peer groups are closer, more familylike. In the last two years, Jewish cultural life has grown more intensive. More young people are going to the synagogue. I try to go to the synagogue every Saturday.

I think it is important to learn Hebrew, because it's the language of the Bible and Jews should know it. I was in Israel once already and I'm longing to return one more time. I think young Jews from all over Eastern Europe should go to Israel once in their lifetime. They will learn more about the origins of the Bible and where those events took place.

— Judit

György Davidovics, seventeen years old, grew up in the small town of Nyíregyháza, and just recently moved with his parents to Budapest. His mother comes from a Hasidic family while his father comes from an Orthodox one.

It was difficult to be a Jew in Nyíregyháza since there were only a small number of Jews. Still for a long time there were enough people to gather for prayer on Saturdays, but lately even this has become impossible. There was no Jewish community there, and anti-Semitism was practically unheard of or at least barely noticeable. Generally the people accepted the fact that I was a Jew and were happy to see my strong commitment to religion.

Living there, my parents grew a little less intense for some time in their religious beliefs. But we started living a religious life when we moved here to Budapest. My grandparents have influenced my strong religious beliefs as has an old friend of the family's whom I met when I started to learn Hebrew. At the beginning my parents found my strong interest in religion somewhat weird, but later on they understood and now they are absolutely content about it. For me Judaism in the first place means religion, and in the second place the culture. Nevertheless, I don't think you can really separate these two concepts. Both inseparably belong to me being a Jew, religion and culture.

Jewish culture is growing stronger. Why, I don't know, but thank God there are more Orthodox and Reformed students going to Hebrew school. And as a result of this, more of them apply to go to the Jewish high school, and more young people are going to the synagogue too. But what the future will bring is anybody's guess.

György with his friends enjoying an afternoon of games at the Kazinczy synagogue (left) and György and his pals (right).

György, fourteen years old, and Andras Klein, eight years old, live with their parents in what was known as the Jewish quarters before the war in Budapest.

I wasn't born in Hungary. I was born in the USSR, in Uzgorod. My mom was born there, too, but my dad was born a little farther away in a small village. Our whole family comes from there. There is quite a big difference between Jewish life there and here. In the USSR we were forbidden to practice religion, and only lately has worship been permitted due to perestroika.

I'll have my Bar Mitzvah on May sixth. I'm looking forward to it because this is the time when a boy is initiated into manhood. From then on I will be looked upon as an adult Jew.

In Hebrew school I like studying Jewish history, mainly because there is a lot to be learned and I think much of it can be applied in practice to our daily lives. In my regular school there are a few class-mates who sometimes call me "Jew." Fortunately the majority of my friends don't do this.

— György

I like going to Hebrew school. It is interesting to learn what religion is all about and to learn to read Hebrew. If I had my Bar Mitzvah and couldn't read Hebrew, I'd be ashamed and that would be embarrassing. Before the teacher comes in, we do play a little but we also have to learn so that we are not dumb.

I actually like all of the Jewish holidays, because my parents usually take me out of school for them for a few days. This in itself is a good thing. I like the joyous holidays more than the fasting ones. On Passover we have to eat a lot of matzo, but I'd rather eat pasta. But we can't eat pasta on Passover because it is made with some leavening ingredients in it.

— Andras

György and Andras on their way
home from Hebrew school.

Gabor Fleischer, twelve years old, lives with his mother and younger sister near the former Jewish ghetto in Pest. Budapest is a city separated by the Danube River. On the north side of the river bank is Buda and on the south side is Pest.

My father is Jewish and my mother is not. My father used to be more involved in Jewish culture, but now he only participates when there are holidays or special gatherings, like last week we went to the Passover Seder at the synagogue. But I feel more like a Jew, even though I live with my mother and study Christian history at school.

I think it is important for everyone, not just Jewish children, to learn about what happened to the Jews during the war. It makes you aware of the possibility of such terrible happenings. Even now when I go in the courtyard with my friends, I never play army.

Gabor enjoying a piece of matzoh
during the Passover seder (left)
and playing in his apartment
complex (below).

Agi, fourteen years old, Eszter, thirteen years old, and Kati Suranyi, nine years old, live with their parents in Budapest. They are one of the few Orthodox families in Hungary.

Our home is quite religious. We keep kosher and don't go to school on the High Holidays. We also observe the Sabbath, and on it we don't write or ride but only read, talk and pray. Our school goes on a lot of trips on Saturdays, and I have to miss these. But compared to the Orthodox in Israel, we aren't so religious. For me, being Orthodox isn't difficult since this is all I've known since my childhood.

— Agi

I've grown up in an Orthodox home and when I have my own family I will keep kosher and have an Orthodox household as well. But some things, such as wearing the long black kaftan and boys having earlocks, are too much for me. The Orthodox who wear such clothes limit themselves too much. They don't go to the theater or to the movies. I don't like this, because it's necessary to enjoy other parts of daily culture.

— Eszter

I'm going to Hebrew school so I will learn why we celebrate holidays and know what was going on long ago. My favorite things to do there are singing Hebrew songs and reading Hebrew books. I'm the youngest in the family, so I will recite the Four Questions, a special prayer said on Passover at our Seder.

— Kati

Kati, Agi and Eszter (left to right) on their way to Hebrew classes at the Nephinhaz synagogue (left) and in a downtown Budapest doorway (right).

Julie Vajda, fourteen, lives with her parents and younger sister in Budapest. Her father is Jewish and her mother is not.

When I write, it is often in a diary. I am a maniac about keeping memories. I have a whole cupboard full of my memories written down on little pieces of paper. I like to read what I thought about years ago. Only yesterday, I read something I wrote when I was eight years old and I thought how stupid I was.

At school I particularly like twentieth-century history. So many things happened in the twentieth century that will affect my life and many generations after. I feel one should know his past to be able to control his future. I'll learn Hebrew as long as I can. There is a lot to learn, and I won't be able to learn everything in four or five years. Our teacher is great. He's not so strict. If you do something he told you not to do, he doesn't bite your head off. Even though I go to synagogue, I don't believe in God. I believe in biology. I believe in the feeling, the feeling of being Jewish. It's something great. But in God, no. That's a different question.

I hope the resurgence in Jewish culture is going to keep growing. I don't think anyone can stop this. But no matter what, the feeling that you are Jewish still cannot be destroyed, even for yourself. The feeling is inside of you forever.

Julie relaxing after school.

Afterword   Jewishness for most of the youth I met was a very personal thing and could not be defined easily. They felt Jewish, saw themselves as Jews, wanted others to see them as Jews, and wanted a chance to be able to raise their future families Jewish. Yet Jewish culture for these children was very different from what it was for their parents only a generation before, whose own parents were afraid to make their religion public.

Not knowing their Jewish heritage or even family history was a problem for many of the youth I met. Many of the Jews who returned to their homes after the war changed their names to sound more Czech, Polish, or Hungarian. They disappeared into the fabric of everyday life and completely assimilated into the dominant culture. So these youth's parents grew up with little or no knowledge of their Judaism. What could they possibly pass down to their children of the seventies and eighties?

While I expected the people of each country to see their lives differently because of the differences in their culture and government, I found that because of similar histories they really weren't that different after all. There were, of course, differences unique to each Jewish population in each country.

In East Germany the Jewish population is so small you must visit East Berlin to observe any kind of Jewish life. Glasnost has shattered the Berlin Wall, and the society and Jewish community is in a state of change. Whether or not there will be a viable Jewish community in East Berlin in ten years will largely depend on whether the young Jewish families emigrate or stay and help build a democratic country.

Jewish children in Czechoslovakia, Poland, and Yugoslavia were particularly affected by a complete loss of Jewish identity. Only recently have the children and their parents begun to publicly assert their search for this Jewish culture.

In Bulgaria and in cities like Kosič, Gyöngyös, and Rijeka, Jewish life for the young is virtually nonexistent outside the home. Unlike the large cities where Jewish culture is experiencing a kind of renaissance, Jewish life in the small cities is vanishing. In these places is it the influence of a close grandparent that carries on the culture. The grandparents represent a world before World War II that was often cloaked in mystery, and spoken of in terms of the tragedies suffered during the Holocaust. But as more and more years distance the grandparents from that period they have begun to speak more openly about their lives before, during, and after the war. Their stories, cuisine, photographs, songs, books, and other memorabilia have created a Jewish world that these children have never known.

Though knowledge or interest in Judaism was often marginal among the children, in every country except Bulgaria they spoke in graphic terms of what happened to their grandparents and other Jews during the war. Because these children live in the countries that witnessed the destruction of Eastern European Jewish culture, it is impossible for them to forget or become insensitive to the Holocaust.

In Bulgaria, where the Jews were not transported to any extermination camps, the youth remember the Holocaust not in terms of personal tragedies, but in how the Bulgarian people helped save the Jews.

In all of Eastern Europe it is becoming increasingly difficult for parents to keep their children unaware of their Jewish heritage. In Yugoslavia, a large traveling museum exhibition on the history of the Jews in that country has stirred the Jewish community to reexamine its Jewish consciousness. And in Hungary there are more Jewish youth groups and Hebrew schools than since before the war.

And most curious of all, in Poland in the last six years Jewish culture has enjoyed such a renaissance among the Catholics that it has swept along many Jewish families that had kept their Jewishness a virtual secret for twenty years. Ironically parents are now discovering their culture along with their children.

A heavy oppressive door has been unlocked allowing a new political freedom in Eastern Europe, and youth — Jew and non Jew — are dancing with the hope of a brighter future. But, sadly, for the Jewish youth this feeling of freedom is tempered with the reality that they are so few and that along with their voices of hope and reason the voices of ignorance and anti-Semitism are also becoming louder.

A father of one of my Polish interviewees put it plainly, "Because the Jews almost disappeared that is why every Pole has a hole, something missing in their physical and personal landscape. This resurgence provokes a fascinating situation."

And one Jewish girl said it most eloquently: "And yet somehow we still are startling the world."

— Y. S.